THINKUPMAN PRESENTS: THE STRANGEST SECRET

THINKUPMAN PRESENTS: THE STRANGEST SECRET

by Earl Nightingale

Reintroduced by Thinkupman:
Classic Wisdom for Everyday People

ELM HILL

A Division of
HarperCollins Christian Publishing

www.elmhillbooks.com

Thinkupman Presents: The Strangest Secret

Published in Nashville, Tennessee, by Elm Hill, an imprint of Thomas Nelson. Elm Hill and Thomas Nelson are registered trademarks of HarperCollins Christian Publishing, Inc.

Elm Hill titles may be purchased in bulk for educational, business, fund-raising, or sales promotional use. For information, please e-mail SpecialMarkets@ ThomasNelson.com.

Library of Congress Cataloging-in-Publication Data

Library of Congress Control Number: 2018965866

ISBN 978-1-400324583 (Paperback)
ISBN 978-1-400324590 (Hardbound)
ISBN 978-1-400324606 (eBook)

ABOUT THINKUPMAN

Thinkupman is your "Success Superhero" with one single mission: to make YOU successful! Naysayers believe that success is only for the chosen few and that the rest should be satisfied with a mediocre life. Thinkupman doesn't believe so! He knows that everyone, including YOU, has the potential to achieve success.

But what's stopping most people? Only one thing: ignorance.

Thinkupman believes that ignorance is the root of all evil. In fact, it is the main reason behind most wars, violence, racism, and unhappiness we face today.

Remember how ignorance once led us to believe that the earth was flat, that smoking (cigarettes) was the best way to relieve pregnancy constipation, and that wireless communication was just crazy talk? We now laugh at these beliefs but back then, people were imprisoned and even sentenced to death for standing up against them.

Thinkupman is here to eradicate ignorance by reintroducing Self-Help materials catered toward our younger generation.

Thinkupman foresees that at the end of his mission, humans will look back at concepts such as war, racism, and violence as foolish dogmas of the past, born from ignorance, and wonder how we ever supported them.

But until then, he needs YOU to be successful!

Are YOU ready for success?

Are YOU ready to unleash your true potential?

Are YOU ready for Thinkupman?

Thinkupman is ready for YOU.

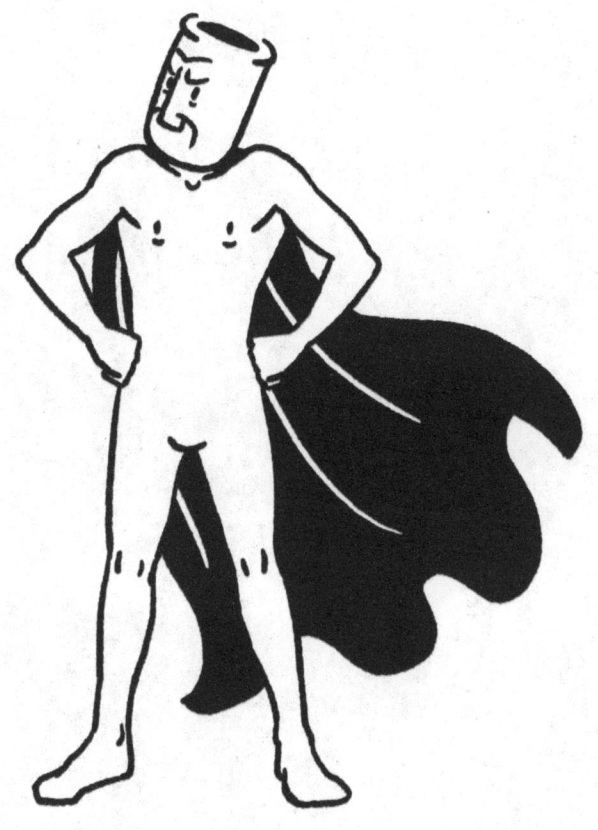

"Ignorance is the root and stem of all evil."

- *Plato*

CONTENTS

CHAPTER I

WHAT'S WRONG WITH PEOPLE TODAY, DOC?

S psttt.... Want to be let in on a secret? This secret is unusual, offbeat, downright strange. In fact, it's one of the **strangest secrets** we've come across. This **secret** is so powerful it could completely transform the way you look at life and your future.

In fact, if you take the time to truly understand this secret and apply it to your life, you will achieve whatever you want—lookout, there's no stopping you once you begin!

Eager to know what this secret is? Good. Listen up....

Let's say there's a group of 100 people—young adults, all around twenty-five years old. Perhaps this group includes the future-you and your friends. All of you have had the same opportunities and advantages;

you're now standing shoulder-to-shoulder, at the starting line of a brand-new life.

But here's the interesting part: although each one of you have different aspirations, one common belief binds you all. What is this belief? Each of you truly believe that you're going to be successful in life!

Sounds promising. But how will things pan out? Let's climb inside our mental time machine and fast-forward to forty years ahead. They say "Time flies," right? Well in our thought experiment, you and your friends are now sixty-five years old. All 100 of you. You're now retired and reflecting on all the achievements in your life.

There are a lot of years between age twenty-five and age sixty-five; that's certainly enough time to look back and admire your many accomplishments, right? As ambitious as you and your friends were at twenty-five, you'd imagine that most of you would have achieved success.

But guess what. Here's the truth:

Out of 100 people, only five people would have eventually made the cut!

Imagine that—we started with a group of 100 people—bright-eyed, confident young adults, but in the end, only five are living the life they dreamed.

Five.

You can count the successes on one hand, don't you know. You're probably wondering—*Why only five?* Why did the others fail? How did they lose that energy, that spark that they had when they were twenty-five? What happened to their dreams, their plans, and their hopes? And perhaps, being the 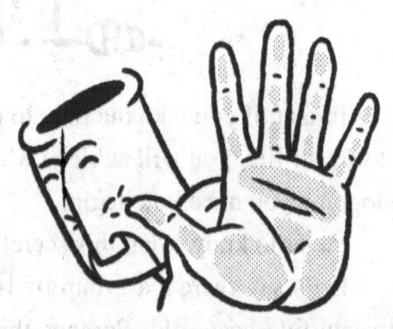 smart reader that you are, you'll reflect on the most important question of all: If each of these 100 young people had envisioned a certain kind of life for themselves, why is there such a wide gap between what they planned and what they eventually accomplished?

That, dear reader, is what we call **the strangest secret**.

A few years ago, a reporter asked the late Nobel Peace awardee, Dr. Albert Schweitzer, a question that made history. Why did this question make history? Because of Dr. Schweitzer's reply.

Reporter: "Doctor, what is wrong with people today?"

The great doctor was silent for a moment and then....

Dr. Schweitzer: "People simply don't think!"

"Most people would rather die than think and many of them do!"
- *Bertrand Russell*

Chew on that. Do you agree with Dr. Schweitzer? Do people today walk, talk, work, love, and sleep all day long ... without thinking?

This is what we need to talk about today.

"Why now?" you ask, your brain turning facts at the speed of lightning. "With all respect to the good Dr. S., humans have done quite well for themselves," you argue, "We've even come close to colonizing another planet—it looks like people are thinking quite a lot!"

Sure, okay. I hear you. And you're right, in many respects. Absolutely, this modern age we live in is a golden age. Humanity has worked hard—for thousands of years—getting us to this level of comfort and ease. Today, there is abundant opportunity for all humans to not only survive, but also thrive. And yet, dear reader, people are simply not thinking.

Why do we say that?

Because, when we take a group of 100 people all aged twenty-five and give them equal advantages, all of them do not become equally successful. As young adults, our cohort of 100 youngsters are eager to begin life's race. They're convinced that they're going to be successful. Bursting with enthusiasm, their energy is infectious, just like yours is when you have an idea.

Chomping at the bit to explore and conquer life, there's a sparkle in their eyes and they hold themselves upright and strong. In our youth, life appears to be an exciting adventure.

But we know what happens, don't we? Most of their stories have an unhappy end. Let's crunch the numbers for our golden youngsters turned golden years. And heads up—we can't crunch the numbers without crunching some dreams: ninety-five dreams to be exact.

Yep, by the time these folks are blowing out their sixty-five birthday candles, only one will be rich and four will be financially independent!

And the rest?

Five will still be working—and worse, fifty-four will be broke, dependent upon others to provide for life's necessities. They ask their family, friends, children, even grandchildren for assistance.

We bet you wouldn't want to be in this last category—nobody would!

Which brings us again to the question: Why did so many of those people fail? What really happened here? And most important of all: How can you, dear reader, make sure that you're in the top 5 percent; how can you ensure you're in the group that succeeds?

The answer follows....

CHAPTER II

THE DEFINITION OF SUCCESS

G ood. You're still reading. That can only mean that you want to learn how to be successful … and that's wonderful! Congratulations. I haven't scared you off yet. You're one step closer to being in the 5 percent of successes. You're on the right path, so keep going.

But first, what exactly is "success"?

If we don't understand the concept of success, we won't get very far—it's like trying to drive without knowing what "driving" means. Here is the best definition of success we've been able to find: success is the progressive realization of a worthy ideal.

Pretty sweet, right? Imagine that. Success is achieved when one is on the path that they deem worthy. In other words, success is when an individual who knows what they want to do works towards achieving their dream.

Let's take Jen, for example. Jen is an elementary school teacher and she's successful. Why? Because she wanted to teach and that's exactly what she's doing now. Or take Sam. He has just set up his own business, but we can say that he's already achieved success, because he always wanted to be an entrepreneur.

In the same way, Lara, a sales manager, is already successful because she has decided to become the best sales manager in her company and is now following a plan of action to get there.

This is the definition of success.

Beautiful, isn't it?

When a person is working toward a worthy goal or purpose that they've decided upon, they have already achieved success.

Wait, what? "That can't be right," you say.

Yes, it's true. Having a goal or purpose is something that the individual deliberately decided to achieve. Now you're probably thinking, "Wow! If this is success, it's pretty easy to achieve!"

Yet we know so many people who fail in life! Why?

Get this: only one out of twenty people have a goal and work towards it with purpose and determination. The rest don't have a goal or have a goal they don't actively work towards. And they're—sorry to say—failures.

Rollo May, a famous psychiatrist, wrote a wonderful book called *Man's Search for Himself*. The book is a great read; however if you only read one sentence from the book, let it be this: "The opposite of courage in our society is not cowardice … it is conformity."

Whoa. Just sit with that for a moment.

You're in high school or college, so you deal with the seduction of conformity all the time. But guess what—adults deal with conformity as well. When you conform, you don't have to make your own decisions or make your own way. You don't stand up for what you believe in, you simply do as the rest do.

Conforming sounds easy, right?

The opposite of the person who is brave and fearless is not the one who is a coward—rather, it is the person who conforms to society, somebody who follows the herd, just like sheep do.

Baaaaaa! Yikes. Are you a sheep or a human?

When people try to be like others, blindly following other people and practices, they're not going to go very far in life.

"Be careful when you follow the masses. Sometimes the M is silent."
- *Ashwani Dagar*

"OUR GREATEST WEAKNESS LIES IN GIVING UP.
THE MOST CERTAIN WAY TO SUCCEED IS ALWAYS
TO TRY JUST ONE MORE TIME."
-THOMAS A. EDISON

Imagine if all the great inventors like Thomas Edison, James Watt, and the Wright brothers never dared to think creatively or challenge human limitations. Imagine if they just did what everybody else was doing—the world would still be sitting in the dark, right?

No lightbulbs, cameras, movies, trains, planes, and all the other wonderful things these inventors contributed to humanity.

If these legends conformed, human progress would have come to a standstill. If we don't think for ourselves, if we follow others without knowing why and where we're going, we will fail.

And so once again, 95 out of 100 people do fail. Are you beginning to see why?

Consider this: we learn to read when we're seven. By the time we turn thirty, we know how to earn money and make a living. Some of us may even be supporting a family. And yet, by the time we turn sixty-five, we still haven't learned how to become financially independent in one of the richest countries ever to exist.

Insanity, right?

Why?

How does this happen?

Conformity happens.

We become just like the next person. And by conforming, we're making the biggest mistake of our lives. We're acting like the people in the group who don't succeed—we become one of the 95 percent who fail.

And who wants to be in that bunch, anyway!

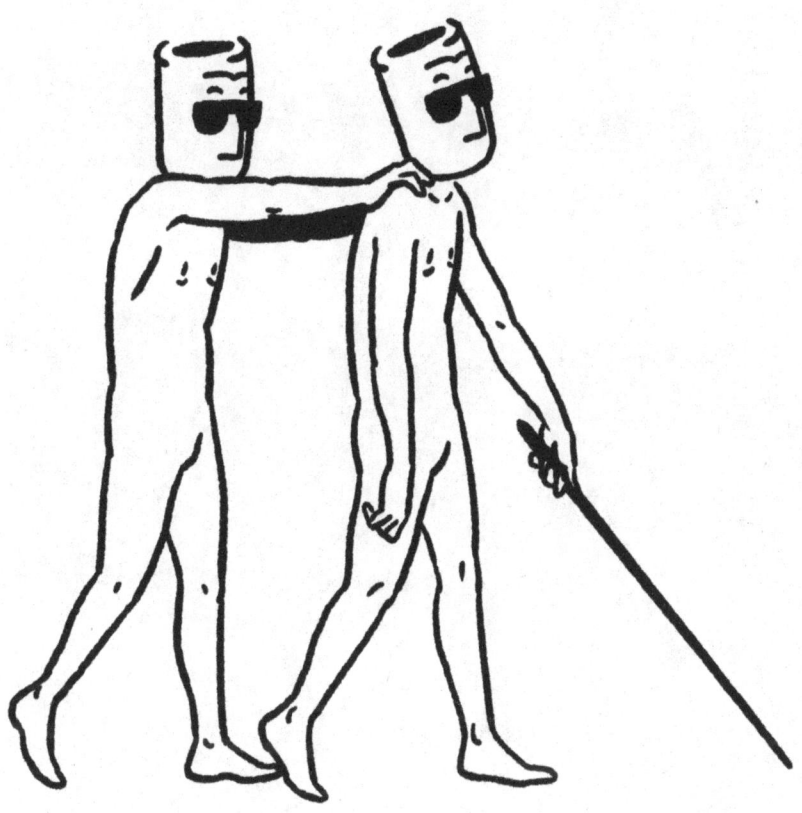

CHAPTER III

GOALS

Have you ever thought to yourself—"Life is so unfair!"? Perhaps this thought struck you when you were wondering why some people work hard and honestly their entire lives and yet achieve nothing, while other people hardly work at all and yet get everything!

It's almost as if the people who get everything have a magic touch. You've probably heard the saying—"Everything they touch turns to gold," or the "Midas touch," right?

Have you noticed the snowball effect of success? That is, successful people tend to become even more successful, while someone who's a failure generally continues to remain a failure? It's strange, but true. Why does this happen? Is there someone up there rolling a dice and randomly deciding who becomes successful and who doesn't?

Nope, I don't think so.

The difference, dear reader, lies in having goals.

People who have goals succeed, because they know where they're going. It's that simple. On the other hand, people who fail believe that they have no control over their lives. "I can't help it," they say. "My life is shaped by external circumstances, by outside forces. Don't blame me, blame my fate."

Boo hoo. Don't cry for these folks. They have more control and power than they realize. These people do nothing to improve their situation, because they assume that they have no say in what happens to them. The result?

They keep failing—because they're caught in a vicious cycle.

"People will choose to blame their circumstances on fate or bad luck.
Very few will admit it's mainly the choices they have made." - *Unknown*

Let's change tacks here with a question: Would you board a ship with no captain and no crew?

Nope. We don't think so.

Imagine a ship whose voyage is completely mapped out down to the last nautical mile. The captain and the crew know where they're going, which route to take, and how long it will take for them to get there.

This ship has a definite goal—and guess what, 9,999 times out of 10,000, this ship will reach its destination—you can bet on that!

Now, let's take another ship. This one is just like the first, except for one major difference. This ship doesn't have a crew or a captain. Nor does it have a destination or a defined goal. In fact, we're just going to raise the sails, cast off, and exit the harbor outward bound.

Where will this ship go? Who knows! In fact, will it even go any-where? Will it leave the harbor? Will it even leave the dock? Before you

can say, "Ship ahoy!" you can imagine how this ship will be adrift for hours, days, weeks, years … forty-five years even … until the passenger aboard that ship is say, sixty-five years old?

If it gets out of the harbor success-fully (which you and I both agree is highly improbable), it will either sink or wind up on a deserted beach—a broken, lost thing.

Forget about going far: this ship won't get anywhere, because we haven't set a destination for it and guided it there. Funny enough, human beings work in the same way. We cannot get ahead if we don't have a course, or a fixed goal and constant guidance.

"Without a goal, you can't score."
- Casey Neistat

Now, you wonder, "If this were true, wouldn't most of the human population be roaming around lost and miserable, since only five people out of every 100 succeed? Well, most people may not be happy or successful, but they're scraping by and making a living. How is this possible?

As humans, we have formed a society and made rules that protect the weak. By having fixed structures, the strong can of course win; but at the same time, we can prevent the weak from losing.

Think of our society as a fleet of ships during wartime.

This fleet has fast ships and slow ships. But to stay the course, the entire fleet must always move together and never break formation. Thus, the fastest ship reduces its speed to a pace that the slowest ship can keep up with.

In the same way, by having these rules and structures, our society has slowed down to protect its weakest link. That's why it's quite easy to make a living today.

Surprised? But it's true.

It takes no smarts or talent to earn money or support a family today. Society has provided us with a safety net—and most of us are resting comfortably on this plateau of so-called "security."

What's that? You say you want to succeed and not just "get by"? You want to rise above the baseline, the low bar, the mediocrity?

Great! If you want to succeed, you must decide how high above this plateau you want to aim.

Your success or failure depends entirely on you.

What makes us say this with conviction?

Throughout history, wise men, prominent thinkers and philosophers have argued and disagreed over a great many things. However, they are all in complete and unanimous agreement over one point—the key to failure and the key to success is one and the same: we become what we think about.

"YOU BECOME WHAT YOU THINK ABOUT"
- NAPOLEON HILL

CHAPTER IV

WE BECOME WHAT
WE THINK ABOUT

We become what we think about. Remember this statement, dear reader, because this is **the strangest secret**. Now you may be wondering, "Why do you call it strange, and is it really such a secret?"

As a matter of fact, it isn't so secret after all. In fact, this powerful truth has been out there all this while! It was first referred to by some of the world's earliest wise men. The Bible, too, contains this truth.

But despite this, very few people have learned it or even understand it. And that's why it's strange. This truth can completely transform your life—and you would think that by now, people would have known all about it, practice it, and live it.

But for some strange reason, it remains practically a secret.

At the start of this chapter, we mentioned that a great many wise souls throughout history have spoken about this secret—but who exactly are these people?

To begin with, the great Roman emperor, Marcus Aurelius, once said, "A man's life is what his thoughts make of it." Simply put—your life is made up by your thoughts. As if each thought is a brick, and brick by brick—you have the brick road of your life.

The former British Prime Minister Disraeli also knew about the secret. He once said, "Everything comes if a man will only wait ... a human being with a settled purpose must accomplish it, and nothing can resist a will that will stake even existence for its fulfillment."

In other words, what he meant was: If you wait, everything will come to you. If you have a set purpose in life, you must work towards it, and no obstacle will stop someone who is willing to devote their life to the fulfillment of their goal.

The American philosopher and psychologist William James has also echoed this thought and outlined a simple way to realize our ambitions. To make our goals and dreams come true, William James encourages us to act as if our goals and dreams have already come true.

Why should we do this? Because when we do so, our goals and dreams will become an inseparable part of us, they will be woven into the fabric of our lives. And soon our habits and emotions will follow these goals, and our belief in our goals and our capability to achieve them will grow stronger and stronger.

But—

And there always is a "but," right?

William James presents us with a warning. He reminds us to choose one or two goals and focus on them exclusively. Don't chase too many dreams with equal fervor and passion. Because then, you will end up realizing none!

"Person who chases two rabbits catches neither."
- *Confucius*

Let's take two more examples.

An old friend, Dr. Norman Vincent Peale, put it this way: "If you think in negative terms, you will get negative results. If you think in positive terms, you will achieve positive results."

Isn't that a simple and beautiful way to tell **the secret**? Think positively and get favorable results!

The writer, George Bernard Shaw, believed in going after dreams too. He said, "People are always blaming their circumstances for what they are. I don't believe in circumstances. The people who get on in this world are the people who get up and look for the circumstances they want, and if they can't find them, make them."

So remember that and write it down somewhere safe, dear reader. Don't blame your circumstances; get out there and change them. Successful people pursue the circumstances they want, and if they can't find them, they create them!

There you have it. Pretty clear now what **the secret** is, isn't it? Sort of like "You are what you eat," but in this case, "You are what you think." We become what we think about.

A person who thinks about a goal is going to reach it, because that's what he or she is thinking about. On the other hand, people who have no goals and don't know where they're going are plagued by confused thoughts. This, in turn, creates a life of frustration, fear, anxiety, and worry.

And what about the people who think about … nothing?

Well, they become … nothing!

Dear reader, if you want a happy and successful life, start thinking hard about what you want to become. There's no magic involved; it's that easy.

"Just like every food you eat affects your body, so does every thought."
- *Thinkupman*

CHAPTER V

As Ye Sow —
So Shall Ye Reap

“What should I plant?” a young farmer wonders, staring at her newly purchased plot of land. “I could grow kiwis or maybe plums, or perhaps some corn or spinach?” she muses aloud, surveying the rich, fertile soil.

The land looks back at her but doesn't say a word. In fact, it doesn't care what is planted in its soil. That decision is up to the young farmer.

But whatever the young farmer decides to sow, the land will nurture it and return it in abundance.

The mind, dear reader, is just like this farmland. It doesn't care what you plant in it, but it will return what you plant. What does our young farmer decide to plant?

She decides to plant two seeds—one of corn and the other of nightshade, a deadly poison. She waters the plants and takes care of them diligently. Now, what do you think happens?

The land doesn't care what is planted in it. It does not discriminate between corn or poison—it nurtures poison just as well as it nurtures corn and returns both in wonderful abundance.

Remember the saying, "As you sow, so shall you reap?"

This truth applies to life in general, just like it applies to the farmland. The young farmer had planted seeds of corn and poison and the land gave her back corn and poison.

Why is the story about the farmland important now? Because, dear reader, the human mind is like the farmland.

In fact, the mind is far more powerful and fertile and far more incredible and mysterious than the land—but it works in the same way. Just like the land, the mind doesn't care what you put in it—you could plant thoughts of success or failure.

For example, you could plant a well-defined, worthwhile goal in your mind. Or you could sow thoughts of confusion, misunderstanding, fear, anxiety, and so on.

Here is the most important part to remember: whatever you plant in your mind, your mind must, and will, return it to you. But wait a minute—if it's so easy, why isn't everyone planting seeds of success in their mind?

The problem is that we're all born with a mind—it's standard operating equipment—like getting an engine when you buy a car. But unlike a car, you don't have to pay for your mind: you get it for free.

If you've ever gotten a freebie, you know what happens—we don't think much of it and we certainly don't treasure it. In the same way, since we got our mind for nothing, we don't pay it as much importance as we should.

Unfortunately, we only value the things we pay a price for.

And you know what's funny? We value the things we pay a lot of money for, but in fact, those things are not really that valuable. Everything that is precious and worthwhile in life we receive, all for free!

What are these, you wonder?

They are our minds, our souls, our bodies, our hopes, our dreams, our ambitions, our intelligence, our love for our family, children, and country. These, dear reader, are priceless possessions—and these are all free.

"But what about the things we pay money for?" you ask. Believe it or not, those things are actually very cheap and can be replaced at any time.

Think about that for a minute. A rich man can lose his business overnight and yet build another successful business from scratch, all over again. In fact, we know of many people who have done just that in real life.

Even if our home burns down, we can build another one. But can we go to the supermarket and get another mind, or another body? No!

The things we got for free—like our mind, our bodies—these we can never replace. Let's reflect on this again, because it's crucial to our success. Our mind is such a powerful tool—it can do all kinds of wonderful things.

And yet, what do we do?

We give it small, simple tasks to accomplish. It's like having a supercomputer at home and using it just to read your e-mail. Seems silly, doesn't it?

"True happiness involves the full use of one's power and talents."
- *John W. Gardner*

Now, dear reader, it's time to make a very important decision—in fact, the most important decision of your life because it will shape your future.

Your mind is the fertile soil, and you are the young farmer. It's time for you to make a choice. Decide now:

What do you want to do with your mind?

What goal do you want to plant?

Do you want to excel at a job?

Do you want to rise through the ranks in your company or in your community?

Do you want to become rich?

Once you decide on a goal, all you must do is plant this seed of thought in your mind, pay attention to it, and work steadily toward it every day. And very soon, you will discover that your goal has become a reality—the thought you planted in your mind would have come true.

In fact, there's no way it cannot come true.

It's guaranteed, because this is the law.

Just like we have laws for other things, like gravity. Say, if a person jumps from a building, will they go down or up? Of course, they will go down because that's how the laws of gravity work. And it's the same with the other laws of nature, too—they always work. They cannot and will not change.

In the same way, the law of planting seeds in your mind which says "What you sow in your mind and work toward will eventually come true" always works too.

Try it for yourself and see; that's the only way you'll believe it! Perhaps you're shouting back at these pages and saying, "This all sounds well and good, but how do I start?"

First, answer the question—"What is my goal?"

Then take a deep breath, relax, and think about your goal positively.

What do I mean by that? Well, if your goal is to write a book, picture yourself having already written the book. What would you do once you've finished writing this book? Imagine yourself doing those things.

Go on, try it now. Think of what you want to achieve and picture yourself having already achieved it and living the life you want.

Have you ever noticed someone and wondered: What makes a person that person? Is it their face, their body, their mannerisms? But what if these changed with cosmetic surgery or other manipulations—then who exactly is that person? That person, and every other person, is the sum of their thoughts.

Who are you right now?

Let's find out here and now.

At this moment, you have more than a million thoughts in your head. Think of every thought you have like a piece of a puzzle in a million puzzle set. Each thought takes up valuable real estate, doesn't it?

Put all the thoughts together, like puzzle pieces, and the completed picture comes into focus before you. Now, this realization is important because it reveals how much power our thoughts have.

For example, all of us have often complained about our situation in life—but we are where we are because that's where we feel we deserve to be, or that's where we really want to be. Of course, this is often hard to admit to ourselves.

"I always wonder why birds choose to stay in the same place
when they can fly anywhere on the earth, then I ask myself the
same question." - *Harun Yahya*

If we try telling a poor man, "Sir, you are in this miserable condition now because that's where you feel you should be," we're sure to get a smack in the jaw. But unfortunately (or fortunately, depending on how you see it), that's the plain truth.

We are what we think—nothing else and nobody else is to blame for who we are.

Your thoughts define you—and you will have to face the consequences of your thoughts in the future. What you think today, tomorrow, next month, and next year will shape your life and determine your future.

So, think carefully, dear reader! For you are guided by that powerful tool—your mind! Here's a comparison. Your mind is a great big monster of a machine.

For example, have you ever seen those giant, earth-moving machines that can make even the tallest dinosaur seem like a harmless garden lizard? These incredibly powerful machines can move a hundred tons of dirt at a time!

"All right, this isn't a book about construction," you might say, "so why are we suddenly talking about earth-movers?"

Well, if you've looked closely, you would have noticed a driver perched way up on top, with the wheel in his hands, expertly guiding this beast of a machine by a simple dashboard of controls. That lone driver is responsible for where the machine goes and what it does. And that's strikingly similar to the relationship between you and your mind.

Your mind is like the wonderful earth-moving machine. And you, dear reader, are the sole driver perched on top of this mechanical beast. You have at your control this vast source of energy and power.

But what are you going to do with it? Are you going to put your feet up, fold your hands, and let the machine run into a ditch? Or are you going to grab that wheel firmly with both hands and direct this power toward a meaningful, worthwhile goal?

It's all up to you now.

It's always been up to you.

You're in the driver's seat, handling the vast power that is your mind. You see, the very law that states a person will be successful if they nurture successful thoughts and work toward them also holds true if a person has weak thoughts and nurtures them.

If you don't control your thoughts, you're essentially taking your hands off the wheel—which means you will run into trouble. And when unmanned, that earth-moving machine can do a lot of unintended damage. The same law that helps people become successful and achieve the things they want can also drive them into the gutter. It all depends on how you use this law.

Do you use it to encourage good thoughts that will help you succeed, or to promote bad thoughts that will lead you to ruin and misery? Your choice, dear reader, makes all the difference. And that is **the strangest secret!**

So, what's next? What should you do?

Our advice: Do what the experts have been encouraging us to do since the beginning of time—pay the price—and become the person you want to become.

Yes, we know it's tough paying the price. You want to become the best in your field, but that means you must work long and hard, giving up your movie and entertainment time, and probably not hanging out with your friends as often.

But if you choose to do this, to make those sacrifices, eventually, you'll realize it's not nearly as difficult as living an unsuccessful life. The regrets you live with will be much, much worse. And here's something that is sure to cheer you up: when you decide on a meaningful goal to work towards, you've already become successful in an instant.

Once you set a goal and make the choice to follow it, you've entered that rare group of people who knows exactly where they're going. Imagine that—out of 100 people, you'll immediately become one of the top five—the five destined to succeed!

"But hang on!" you exclaim. "How am I supposed to get there, what am I supposed to do…."

Forget about these questions for a moment. Leave the "how" of it to the power of the universe. Right now, all you need to do is to decide on a worthwhile goal.

The answers will then come to you automatically, at the right time and place. Start today and decide on a goal, dear reader. Indeed, you must. You have nothing to lose—but your whole life to win!

**"IF YOU CAN DREAM IT,
YOU CAN DO IT."**
—WALT DISNEY

CHAPTER VI

THIRTY-DAY ACTION PLAN

You know the secret now, but what should you do next? How can you make this secret work for you and achieve your heart's desire? This is where our thirty-day action plan will help.

All that's required is to follow three simple steps every day and you will soon achieve your goal. Then you will be in that rare 5 percent of people who become what they dreamed.

You will become the best version of yourself, guaranteed! So, ready to begin this exciting journey? Jump aboard then! Success, here we come!

Step One

Write down what you really want more than anything in the world. Not quite sure? No worries, here are a few launching-off points to get started. Perhaps you want money. Maybe you want more money than what you're earning now, or you have a certain amount in your head.

Your goal could be anything—a beautiful home, success at work, a specialized position in life, or a happy family. Think about it and then write it down. But write down exactly what you want. Make sure it's one goal and it's clearly defined. You don't have to show it to anyone but keep it with you and look at it several times a day. Read it to yourself often.

Every morning when you wake up, think about your goal in a relaxed and positive way. Soon you'll discover that you can't wait to get out of bed because now you have something to work for, something to look forward to in life. And as you go about your day, look at the piece of paper with your goal written.

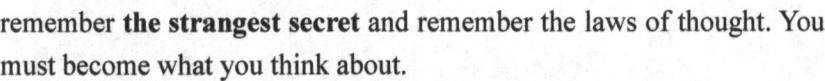

Do the same thing just before you go to bed at night. Maybe you'll even dream about your goal!

Do you have the piece of paper with you right now? Look at it and as you do, remember **the strangest secret** and remember the laws of thought. You must become what you think about.

Are you thinking about your goal now?

If yes, then you'll realize that this goal will soon be yours. In fact, it was yours the moment you decided upon your goal and wrote it down—you're already on the path to achieve it.

Step Two

Get rid of your monsters!

Yes, dear reader, you need to get rid of the biggest monsters that stand between you and your goals—your fears! All of us have worries and fears, especially when it comes to our path in life. But it's time to crush these monsters once and for all. We must stop thinking about them—right now.

But how? It's so difficult, right? Well, we have an easy method to achieve this heroic feat.

Try this: each time a fearful or negative thought comes into your mind, replace it with a mental picture of your positive and worthwhile goal.

As soon as you start worrying, tell yourself, "Let me envision my goal and what it feels like to accomplish it." If you do this every time you think negatively, you will soon make positive thinking a habit.

Of course, there will be times when you'll feel like giving up. We've all been there. This is because it's easier for human beings to think negatively instead of positively. Did you know that? And that's why only 5 percent of people are successful!

"If you don't like what you see in life, choose a different channel."
- *Thinkupman*

You should now think of yourself in that coveted group. You'll become one of the five percent. Think positively and you'll be surprised to see that things will happen according to what you think.

As writer and editor Dorothea Brande says, "Act as though it were impossible to fail." If you think and act like you've succeeded, you will succeed. If you think about your goal everyday—no matter what your goal is—you will be amazed at this new life you've found!

Step Three

"I did nothing and I became successful," has said no successful person ever! That's because success will always depend on the quality and quantity of work you put into achieving your goal. You know that hard work always pays off. But you must also do your best, along with working hard to become truly successful.

Now if you ask people what they want, most of them will say, "We want to make tons of money!" But these people don't understand the law. The only people who make money are the ones who work in a mint! They physically make the coins that we spend. Cha-ching! But how do we get money? We must earn it, of course!

The people who want to "make money" are looking for a free ride. They want something without giving or doing anything in return. What happens to such people? Well of course, they fail in life.

Success is not the result of making money. In fact, it's just the opposite. You earn money when you become successful. If you are successful, then you will be paid for your work and the value you bring to the table. How successful you will become depends on how good your work is!

Most people think about this the wrong way. They understand the law backwards.

Imagine if it's snowing outside and you have a fireplace to keep warm. Those who don't understand this law will stand in front of the fireplace and say, "Give me heat and then I'll add the wood."

Hmmm…. Fireplaces don't work like that. Do you think these folks will ever get warm?

"Give me heat and then I'll add the wood. How many men and women do you know, or do you suppose there are today, who take the same attitude toward life? There are millions."- *Earl Nightingale*

If you're wondering who these people are, look around. There are millions of people in this world who apply this same attitude to life. They all want something … for nothing.

But you, dear reader, understand how fireplaces work, right? We realize that we must put the wood in and light the fire if we expect to get some heat. In the same way, we must put the work in before we expect the money. You must prove that you're useful before you can expect to get paid. But don't think about the money just yet. You shouldn't be concerned about that right now.

All that's required is for you to be of service—build ... work ... dream … create! If you follow through, you'll find that there is no limit to the richness and prosperity that will come to you in life. Do the work and the rewards will be plentiful.

Now, dear reader, you know the three simple steps that will help you achieve any goal you set your heart and mind on. But before you start, we must ask you a very important question: Are you "all in"?

DO. OR DO NOT.
THERE IS NO TRY.
-YODA

Have you decided to do this with all your heart and stick to it, no matter what?

Warning! There will be hurdles along the way, because nothing is easy. But if you have made up your mind to do this, you will achieve your goal! And if, during the first thirty days, you find yourself overwhelmed with negative thoughts, don't worry. Simply start over from that point where you stopped and go on for thirty more days.

And you know what? It will get easier and easier to think positively and soon, it will become a habit! Then one day you will belong to that wonderful group of people for whom nothing is impossible!

Above all ... don't worry! Worry brings fearful thoughts which can cripple you. If you're anxious about doing it all by yourself, don't be! All you must do is know your goal and hold it in front of you, every day.

"And what about the other things I'm worried about," you wonder. Well, that will take care of itself. The universe will see to it. So, follow these three steps for a month and then repeat.

Then repeat again.

The more times you repeat the process, the more it will become a part of you and one day you'll wonder—"How could I have ever lived my life any other way!"

Start living like this and soon riches will be showered on you. More than you ever dreamed! If you're thinking of money, you'll get lots of it. But more importantly, you'll also get peace. You'll be among that 5 percent who live calm, cheerful, and stress-free lives.

So, what are you waiting for?

You now know **the strangest secret** and you know how to make it work for you.

Go on then, take control of your dreams.

Grab life by the horns.

Don't wait—start today.

Start now.

Because remember:

you have nothing to lose. But you have a life to win.

Acknowledgment

You! That's right: I want to acknowledge you for having the discipline to read this book from cover to cover. However, this is just the beginning of our journey. Now, I need to take everything you've learned in this book and apply them in your life. I need you to take **action**.

To start, I encourage you to surround yourself with like-minded friends who share your vision and passion. Jim Rohn stated best when he said, "You are the average of the five people you spend the most time with."

Grab extra copies of this book and share them with your loved ones so they can grow with you! There is nothing more gratifying than sharing success with the people you love the most. Lastly, I'm cheering for you all the way. Don't give up on your dreams. They came to you for a reason. I'll look forward to your success and the person you'll become in the process.

To Your Success,
THINKUPMAN
www.thinkupman.com
⌾ thinkupman